Suede Frunchak

CHP

Life Is…A Journey of Redemption Filled with Unexpected Grace
by Suede Frunchak
Published by Creation House Press
A Charisma Media Company
600 Rinehart Road
Lake Mary, Florida 32746
www.charismamedia.com

Unless otherwise noted, all Scripture quotations are from the New American Standard Bible®, Copyright © 1960, 1962, 1963, 1968, 1971, 1972, 1973, 1975, 1977, 1995 by The Lockman Foundation. Used by permission.

Scripture quotations marked THE MESSAGE are from *The Message: The Bible in Contemporary English*, copyright © 1993, 1994, 1995, 1996, 2000, 2001, 2002. Used by permission of NavPress Publishing Group.

Design Director: Justin Evans
Cover design by Karen Gonsalves

Visit the author's website: Life.is.author@gmail.com

Library of Congress Cataloging-in-Publication Data: 2015948216
International Standard Book Number: 978-1-62998-480-3
E-book International Standard Book Number: 978-1-62998-481-0

While the author has made every effort to provide accurate telephone numbers and Internet addresses at the time of publication, neither the publisher nor the author assumes any responsibility for errors or for changes that occur after publication.

First edition

15 16 17 18 19— 9 8 7 6 5 4 3 2 1
Printed in the United States of America

I recently outfitted my Motorbike. I have a Triumph Speedmaster—which will now have the pronoun *her* or *she*—and not to over-state it, but she is my most prized possession. She might be the only thing that I own that I love. I bought her a new seat, backrest, back rack, and bag. I then spent an hour or so installing the new stuff, took a picture of her, and posted it on Social Media (because that is what we do these days).

As I was working on my Motorbike, Suede called me about writing this book. We talked for a bit, and I returned to my work. These two unlikely connections got me thinking…as much as I can when I tinker with my motorcycle, I have no real skills when it comes to ever actually fixing her. The best I can do, if something seriously goes wrong, is send her to a mechanic. Ultimately, my skills are very limited.

When I met Suede, he was far along his transformational journey. Already clean and sober, he walked into the church I pastor with his lovely wife and beautiful daughter seeking the last part of wholeness—the healing of his soul.

As Father Gregory Boyle so profoundly says, it wasn't long "and the soul found its worth" for Suede. He and I would go for coffee and talk about his soul. We would talk about love, Jesus, and God's hand upon his life.

The day Suede was baptized was a profound one; in Jesus, his soul had found its worth. It was a great reminder that this is why I love being a pastor. Who Suede is and who he is becoming is amazing. His soul has found beautiful life. I get to sit back and intimately see what God is doing in Suede's life.

But here's the thing: no person can do for Suede what Jesus is doing in and through Suede. Like me and my motorbike, I can help him out a bit, but its only Jesus that can transform us. It's like Jesus said, "You are the salt of the earth, but if salt has lost its taste, how shall its saltiness be restored?" (Matt. 5:13).

Suede has been restored, and his story of restoration is one that we all should read. Perhaps, in doing so, you will find your soul's worth.

—DEAN KURPJUWEIT

PASTOR OF NEXT CHRISTIAN COMMUNITY

ST. ALBERT, ALBERTA, CANADA

DEDICATION

This book is dedicated to the hopeless kid.

A special thank you to my wife, daughter, and
mother for being the three constants, the three
rocks in my life…you are my shelter.

And to Elizabeth, my editor. Thank you for softening my
voice for others yet still allowing it to be heard so well.

CONTENTS

Chapter 1

LIFE IS ... CONTROL

I FIND MYSELF HERE, now, nearly thirty and looking back. I look at my priorities, my uncertainties about them, and the ever-elusive faith that I am trying to establish in God. All my life I found it difficult to see past what I could not control. I had faith as a child, as a teenager, that one day when I was an adult I would be in control and life would be a lot more simple; in fact, it was just the opposite.

I find myself today going to church, praying with my wife at night, and reading the children's bible to my daughter before she goes to sleep. We live in a routine that is comfortable but at times uncertain. I work construction, so depending on the season, I never see my family or I always see my family. It's not your typical nine to five lifestyle. I can be gone from 5:00 am before they're awake to 11:00 pm after they go to bed. It's as if my daughter can forget I exist for six days, and then get a glimpse of me on Sunday only to forget about me again by Tuesday.

It's hard once you slip into a mold, into that routine, especially when it's not so much by choice, but rather survival. My wife and I have been together three years and have a two-year-old, and like most newly married couples, money is tight. So, we both sacrifice. We work extra hard during the construction season; my wife takes care of all aspects of the home and our daughter while working her nine to five job, and I just try to stay healthy so I don't miss a day. In winter I struggle to find work because of my resume; it really has held us back in many ways, and makes me question where my job fits in our actual priorities.

It's funny because I was praying with a guy over the phone the other day, on one of those prayer lines (that my mother suggested I call). I was having a hard day, and he prayed something I have never heard before. Now maybe it's because I'm new to this whole, daily God concept, but he prayed for the favor of God to be upon me and my family. It actually kind of blew my mind. Being raised Catholic, I feared God; He was for Sundays. The idea of Him being in control turned me into an internal atheist. But the favor of God—a concept where God actually likes me—that was something completely foreign to me, even though I had heard all the contrary preaching over the years.

See I had this priest, God rest his soul, who always preached God is love. In fact he would end his sermons with "God is love, amen." Every single one. He drilled it into us. He was only ten years older than me, so I tended to listen to him...but I never asked questions. I would always be kind to people, help others, but I never questioned his teachings in comparison to my life. I was a drug addict for a long time. I got hooked after high school and sobered up at twenty-five, and all that time listening to "God is love, God is love"... I never really asked myself, is He?

I have lived a pretty hard life. I mean, I worked every season on the roads, but the winter was always a crap-shoot. I could be in Waikiki, I could be in jail, on the streets, or locked away in a psych ward. My favorite was always rehab. There was always so much hope there. But truth be told, I was a black-out drunk and drug addict, and I never knew what was going to happen or how I was going to hurt. It was a very scary time in my life.

I remember when my daughter was born, being in the shower with my wife as she went through her contractions. Lying with her on the bed minutes before she had our daughter. And as I think back to that one day and look at the past before it, I have to say one thing. God is merciful. At least in my life. To take me from where I was to where I am, with all that I have (though it may be very little in some people's eyes)—God is merciful. That being said, I have to agree with my current pastor and say God is in control, but He is not controlling. And I am beginning to come to terms with that.

Control was always a priority for me. Unrealistic control. It seemed the more I tried to grasp it, the more I slipped. The more I became a drunk and a druggie, the more I lost who I was and the more I believed in the delusions that had become my life. My priorities were unhealthy. My God sense was lost, stunted; it quit developing. The addiction made me a monster, not so much to others, but to myself. It was like someone had trapped me in a little cage inside my head and surrendered the key to a blood sucking demon who had dominion over my entire being. I took the worst of it, but my family felt it too.

God being in control, but not controlling, means He let me make those decisions to the point where I had to get it out of my system. I had to come to a place where I wasn't going to give up any more of my life to the insanity of trying to escape it. I had to face where I was. I had to ask for help because I didn't know what I was doing. I believe that was my first step in faith towards a God that is love because all that time I forgot the first principle...love thy self.

That priest is always going to stay with me. Why?

Because he stuck with me. Through all my problems, he always invited me over to his house for conversations. I was paranoid at times or overly depressed, but he always found a way to give me hope. He even came to visit me in the hospital when no one else would talk to me. He always stayed true to his creed and showed me unconditional love. He taught me lessons and kept my morality in check even when I was in self-destruction mode. He shared things with me—thoughts, desires—that he never shared with anybody else, possibly because I was so constantly elusive. Maybe he thought I wouldn't remember, but I like to think we just had a different kind of friendship. Like that friend you only see once a year, but when you get together it's just honest. His sermons were about *Star Wars*, *Superman*, and his dog, and he was really the biggest geek you would ever meet, but he had this confidence about him where you knew he believed. And even when I had my doubts and disbelief, he would always bring me back to that point where I at least hoped to believe because he was at such a good place with God.

But how do I love myself? How do I love something I can't control? How do I love God? I'm still struggling with those questions, but I know it's all related to purpose—just like my addiction was. Control is something that is exuded excellently by parents, for whatever reason. There is a comfort in being controlled. Guided. It's why religion is so popular. I don't think control is natural for most people; that's why the majority of parents end up botching the job. That's what I'm afraid of with my daughter. As parents, we need to be taught how to control, or at least seem like we're in control, often for the sake of our kids. Today I find anonymous programs and church to be great resources for me in that aspect, as long as I'm actively listening and seeking out the right people for me and my world. I'm not imagining things the way they ought to be, I'm accepting them the way they are. One thing I have found about myself these days is that I am asking a lot more people what they think about my life. And not just the guy next to me in the bar. I am asking trained, educated, successful people for guidance in my life, and it's making a world of difference. I'm tense about my past, but when I say "this was me then, and this is me now, and I still need help," the response is often, "Oh wow! You have made it so far…good for you…you are so strong." A large part of that was giving up control, even if I didn't know it, because I started actually listening to people, and that started to change me.

I was raised in an Eastern Catholic Church that was very close to Orthodox. I went to Roman Catholic summer camp as a kid, met my friend who became a priest, and now I'm in an evangelical church. I worked the whole religious spectrum and felt less and less control as I moved forward, oddly bringing me closer to God. It is, for me, largely about being in control but not being controlling.

One thing I have realized is that spirituality and religion are two very different concepts. But you need both to build faith. Today, my struggles with faith are slowly becoming victories. The ways in which I have overcome my downtrodden past and the journey it took me on, is slowly becoming a positive foundation of overwhelming knowledge to build the rest of my life upon. God is slow. He is patient. But Jesus drew a line in the sand, and I at least had to figure out at some point which side of the line I stood on.

Chapter 2

LIFE IS . . . ASKING FOR HELP

You will often hear anonymous people and religious folk speaking about how they ask for help every day from God. Some even give thanks at night. As for me, I still struggle with this concept, at least to complete it on a truly religious basis.

When I first asked for help, really asked for help, I was lying in bed with all hope lost and a phrase came to me. . . . *Sometimes love isn't enough and all you have is life, but as long as you have life, you live to love again.* And it stuck. I woke up and wrote it down. I used it to get through the first year of my sobriety until I met my wife. Then I used her. Then my daughter. Then my sponsors. Then my church community, and always my mom. See my mom, for the most part, was always there, except for when she wasn't. Oddly enough that's when I sobered up. She always helped me, but she always enabled me. She would pick me up, dust me off, keep me alive . . . and just as I got six months clean, I would fall again. I have been around the program since I was eighteen. I was that bad. Councilors, sponsors, judges, doctors—they couldn't figure out what was wrong with me. Well, they all knew. They knew it was hopeless until I found something worth living for. I found it that night because I asked God for help, and for the first time I really meant it. The next day I met an older lady who gave me a big book, and she said, "Read it because you're a drunk." So, I did, and I got better. Slowly. But it started that day with that phrase, "sometimes love isn't enough," that I kept repeating over and over again until the sick thoughts in my head would dissipate.

Asking for help isn't an easy thing. Especially for addicts. While the action of asking for a handout may be natural, asking someone to help improve your life is daunting. I went through two sponsors before I landed on my current one and two churches before we found the one we go to every Sunday. Today when I ask for help, I ask expecting to do the work. In fact, that is what I am doing right now by writing this book. I'm passing it on. I'm clearing my head. I'm at a place today where I can say, "all right, I can help people." I've seen a lot. I've been through what you have. I know the taste of an alley; I know the unnerving fear of a holding cell before court. I know the first day of rehab; I know the last. I know the chores at a recovery house. I know the first time you speak at an anonymous meeting. I've been there. I've done that. I actually know how it feels to have a gun to your head, a cold steel blade jammed into your flesh, to take a beating, to be hospitalized after a blackout. I skidded through all the low bottoms, and none of it changed until I honestly asked for help, and by honestly, I mean I was willing to change. Surrender. It's the biggest part of change. It's the sole catalyst. It is essential to give up in order to move on.

You hear people talk about surrender in recovery, and that's just what a lot of people do—talk. In fact, it's what I do, but to truly surrender *is* to get on your knees every morning and night and ask for help and to be thankful you received it. I still struggle with this. I still don't like to get down on my knees and humble myself. I figure God loves me anyway, but I fail to show Him a certain respect that I feel, in my heart, He deserves. Just like addiction, I don't know why I do it. Defiance possibly. He has given me so much, but deep down I say, *Well, He hasn't given me this or that*, and it's wrong! I know it's wrong! But I choose to see how much I can get away with before it hits the fan. Even though my relationship with God is actually, finally, existent today, our timing is still off. I still don't completely trust. And that's okay because truth be told, I still feel sorry for myself about all that I went through, and that's just my personal doubt. My pain, my anguish, my regret, and if I know anything, it's that that stuff doesn't go away overnight. It takes a long time to process, and it is always going to stick with me, for the rest of my life. That's why I believe I have to constantly talk about it: go to meetings, go to church, and ask for help. I must always seek council, even when I'm old, because people's opinions, the right people's opinions, matter, and you need opinions that are honest in order to make yourself a better person. You must always improve, because if you're not improving, you're regressing, and that leads to relapse, which leads to loss, failure, and eventually a slow and painful death.

The worst way to die is to die incapable. Many people die incapable due to disease, something beyond their control, at an old age. But how would you feel if you were incapable and dying and had firsthand knowledge that your decisions are what put you there? You drank away your liver; you melted your brain on drugs. *In excess* is addiction. *Go hard or go home* is addiction. *Screw it, I'll do it tomorrow* is addiction. Addiction is a disease. If you are reading this, chances are you, or someone you love, has this disease. And it doesn't go away; it is lifelong, but there is a way out. *"Help!"* It's all you have to say; it's all you have to mean. There's a whole industry out there to help you. Ask a teacher, a pastor, a parent, even a cop. They will all point you in the right direction. But asking for help has to be a daily thing. You must humble yourself and read the signs of your circumstances to know that you are ready to change and to work for that change. It's 50/50, inch-by-inch, and not many people make it because they are afraid of that change. They are afraid to challenge who they are for the sake of themselves. I know I was. But I am living proof it can be done. So are the people in the rooms, the churches, the synagogues . . . better lives can be achieved, but they have to be desired and earned before they can be obtained.

The best part about asking for help is the rewards. Every day I wake up, grab my daughter, and kiss her, I am rewarded. I see my hard work paying off. If I am lucky enough to make love to my wife and wake up the next day holding her, I know I have done something right. The rewards far outweigh the loss. Sure, I think about a drink from time to time, but all I have to do is look at my wedding ring to realize that isn't me anymore. The commitment of asking for help was the first one I was able to make. Oddly enough, it started a chain reaction. The rewards of being helped, helping yourself, being saved by others and by God are overwhelming. I have struggles and hardships like any other person, but unlike before, today, I'm not alone in my struggles. There is an open, honest dialogue between me and countless other individuals; my life is literally an open book. There's nothing to hide, no shame. I don't care what people think, even if they are going to think negatively about me, because I know I am in the right for once in my life. I am standing in the sand, next to Jesus.

Chapter 3

LIFE IS . . . HONESTY

HONESTY IS HARD. That's really all I want to write. But let me expand on that idea. Honesty is an onion with layers. It's about facing fear and peeling away a disillusioned reality. It is about emotions. Finding them, expressing them, and discovering the thoughts behind them. Then it's simply about sharing those thoughts with somebody who is capable. Honesty is about feeling safe. It has a lot to do with trust.

The most honest I could ever be is with God. Because He knows what's going on anyway. But what happens when you don't trust your God? When you say, "No Buddy. I don't believe. You have done this and this and this, and my life sucks because of You. I don't trust You; I don't even want You around"? I did that; it's called abandoning God. Yeah, I honestly did that. I damned God. My grandmother had died, I was going through a mess of family drama, and people were starting to realize I had an addiction. I was young, eighteen, and I literally screamed it out loud. I put a chair through my mother's living room wall and began the hardest eight years of my life. And truth be told, it's still hard today.

See, my family made me feel safe, and when I started to lose that family, I blamed myself and I blamed God. I lost my sense of honesty from all the lies surrounding my addiction, and I lost my faith from watching a family that had been so close, crumble into petty pieces. It hurt, and that's the most blunt emotion, so I dwelled on it, and I became blunt. I turned inward as I entered manhood, afraid of losing, so never gaining. I picked a job that was menial, but well-paying, so I could stay stoned every day. I had sexual relationships that were shallow, short, and manipulative. All those friends I made over the years slowly, one by one, quit talking to me because they were growing up and getting real lives. And there I was, hungover and hungry, thinking it was still 2003, when I was king of the world and God's gift to women.

Honesty is hard. We don't want to hurt, so we don't look at our situation or our past openly. Past relationships, deaths, the things we see as failures and loss, compound in our hearts and turn us away from God. We distract ourselves with substances, addictions, passions, and we forget for a time; but we always seem to remember. To be honest, I don't know how to deal with those memories. I think they are just a part of who we are. I believe it was more about realizing I shouldn't destroy myself over them than it was making them go away. The distractions are good, as long as they're healthy; but the lesson amidst the experience is the priority for my character. What did I learn? Not to give up. It's funny because I just talked about surrender, but I am talking about after you surrender, even if you surrender daily to God. It's about having that resolve to say "No, I'm not going backwards into those emotions or those memories," on a daily basis. It's having the fortitude to look at my past honestly, to look at my situation honestly. But I have to learn from the lesson that was, in order to face the day that is. Rigorous honesty is a part of my program, a part of my life. It is a necessity for me to remember the way I am in order to maintain my sobriety, even if it is painful at times. It gives my daughter a father and my wife a husband. Those memories, the journey, are blessings because they teach me about the reality God wants me to live in and the character He wants me to embrace.

I remember when I got honest. A lot of things started to happen quickly. I had nothing. I moved out of a recovery house and in with my mother. I met my wife; I started a job; then I proposed. We got pregnant, married, and a year later, since it all began we have a daughter, a townhouse, and two cars. God is usually slow, but it was obvious He really wanted me in this situation. And that's the thing, when you get honest with God, He gets honest with you. He restored me; He brought me to a point that in retrospect could have taken multiple years to achieve. That's the reward about being honest. When you're honest, you usually get what you need, not what you want. If I didn't have my wife and daughter, I would be flat out busted on the street again. There is no doubt in my mind. God saved my life by introducing me to my wife. You could not ask for a better, more understanding, down-to-earth person. She's my rock, my earth angel. And I am hers.

So God is merciful; He is love; He is my teacher. He is honest, but not always straightforward. If I didn't go through all my pain, how would I have met my wife? How would I know all of this joy and comprehend my understanding? We're meant to eat it, all of us. Some more than others. Think of those hard lessons as God's sense of humor. It teaches you how to savor the really good times and provides lessons on how to make them last. Today, I learn from my mistakes. Today, I am honest with people, myself, and God on a daily basis. You can't undercut honesty. Truth is truth. If you're a drunk, you're a drunk. If you're a fatty, you're a fatty. Only I can take the necessary steps to get healthy. It's about being honest and accepting the fact that I need to change. That I want more; that I deserve better. People, God, they will all help me get there. In fact, God will work through people to help get me there.

God is merciful; He is love; He is your teacher, but you cannot forsake Him, and you must ask for help. You must begin a relationship in your head and in your heart with something that is greater than you. I know I had to.

Honesty is about facing facts. What are the facts in your life? Is someone enabling you and your addiction? Are you homeless? Are you incarcerated? Are you a hurt teenager that really doesn't know any better? Jails, institutions, and premature death are the facts about addiction. I don't mean to preach, but the real unfortunate bunch are the ones who sober up at sixty or seventy. I've seen them; they wander around in no man's land until they die. Unless they can get a real God sense about them, then they find joy, but most struggle a lot with depression. The fact is it gets harder and harder the longer your run. I used drugs for ten years, was addicted for eight. I smoked my first joint when I was thirteen, didn't touch the stuff again until I was fifteen, then I was hooked. I tried coke when I was sixteen and meth when I was seventeen. I'm blessed that marijuana was my drug of choice, and that I could take or leave the rest in binges, but I, like most every other addict out there, was messing around at a young age. When you talk to most addicts and ask when they started, you're not going to hear twenty-one, twenty-five. You are going to hear fifteen, thirteen, eight. It's one commonality most of us have outside the fact we couldn't or can't stop.

What if my own daughter has to read this book at a young age because she's getting high? What if she has to see where it led me? I would say, "Why, child, would you think yourself any different? It's obviously something you shouldn't be doing. But, it's also between you and God. Like it was for me." I would have to let her be. The choice is always God's, but he chooses to give that choice to her. So, I would have to kiss her and pray, knowing you can always walk in the shadows of your past, but like the daybreak, there is always a sun waiting to warm your skin. There is always hope. And my God is full of hope.

Chapter 4

LIFE IS . . . ACCOUNTABILITY

WHEN I SAY life is accountability, I mean life is built upon your decisions, lessons, and comprehension of those lessons. That's accountability in a plain and simple definition. It's about owning your reality and being willing to stand up for your choices.

If you are in rehab, you are taking the first step in becoming accountable. But it's like looking at the Rocky statue—there are a lot of steps before you get to the top where you're fist pumping. Each step can take days or weeks because it's an emotional illness.

Accountability is one thing I am failing at with my family. My job—it's feast or famine. Our financial situation is putting a strain on our well-being. I am regularly praying, worrying, and praying some more. I know I have to go back to construction to get back on track, but I also know my current job is not sustainable for our future, especially if we ever want to buy a house or take a vacation. I am struggling to solve this problem, but most of the time I turn my worry over to God. I just try to stay accountable to Him and His will—I trust it. I recently thought that maybe God wanted me to help people, so in between internet searches for a winter job, I started putting down some words here and there, and here I am on chapter four. I have no formal training; I have never written a blog or news article, let alone a book, but I am being accountable to Him and my heart, and He is using me to tell a story that may help a few people...something that may give them hope. That's one thing you must have if you are going to be accountable—hope. Being accountable deals with my past, present, and future. It relays my past experiences to the present moment in hopes that I will make a correct decision in the future based upon those experiences.

With recovery, we have to see addiction as our past experiences in relation to whatever moment we are in; and we have to be accountable to our recovery by using our past knowledge to get us by, soberly. We can apply this principle of accountability to any aspect of our lives—physical, spiritual, emotional, or mental; work, wife, friends, or family.

Oddly enough, I knew accountability when I was young. It was drilled into me. I was raised by a single parent as an only child in a large Ukrainian-Canadian family. In one aspect I was accountable to my mother; we were all either of us had. In the other aspect, my extended family was extremely close, and we did a lot as a unit. Confused? Well, it's simple. Day to day I was with my mom, and we were best friends. But on weekends and special occasions, I was with my extended family, and we were all best friends. My mother and I were a relationship within a network, and we flourished until my grandmother passed, and then that network collapsed upon itself. My mother became more controlling, and I became more rebellious, or the other way around. Either way, the accountability I had to that relationship and that network became non-existent, so I could no longer be accountable to myself. And once I lost that, I became an addict.

Some people never have that, the network. And they are thrown to the wolves right out of the gate. That's why the survival rate of addicts and alcoholics is so low. A councilor told me it is one in one hundred, if that. That's how I know that I am a miracle. My life is purposeful again. It is accountable. My accountability began again with my change, and my resolve in that change. Nobody believed I could get sober. Most thought I would be hospitalized the rest of my life with psychosis. But it was giving up that control, asking for help, and being honest that led to my accountable existence here, today. Without those steps, I would still be in a bottom, living within one of the lowest points of my life. It reminds me of Batman when a young Bruce Wayne falls into a well and discovers the bat cave. Alfred descends to recover him and asks, "Why do we fall Master Wayne?" Well it's obviously to become Batman. To become a superhero to ourselves and to those around us. Isn't it? I mean, what's the point if we are not accountable to other people? Life doesn't really matter then, does it? If we had never fallen down the well at fifteen, thirteen, eight-years-old, we would never have known the possibilities of our future, or the fact that they are limitless. We would have never faced that fear that so many are afraid to encounter. We would never have tested the darkness in our hearts, and we would never have had the opportunity to realize that God was with us the whole time, descending to recover us. If God is accountable to me, should I not be accountable to Him?

I know, I had to be able to trust before I became accountable. I had to trust other people and believe that they knew what was best for me. I became accountable to them and through them, became accountable to myself and to a God of my understanding. I remember getting dish duty at my last recovery house. I was accountable to the cook and to the guys for something as simple as clean dishes, but it was huge because it was a necessity. Accountability is about finding your place in this world and claiming it with God, as God-given. For me, it started with dishes. It turned into relationships, and today it's existential. My journey was difficult. You may think a dish soap revolution asinine, but that's what it was for me—revolutionary. That's how simple it can be. It's a simple program. A simple life. It's slow and methodical, peaceful and assuring. Every purpose is meaningful to life, and every life is purposeful.

Impact. An old friend always told me to live a life of impact. If you're going to be accountable, then be accountable to others, God, and yourself, not just yourself. If Bruce Wayne was never haunted by the bats he saw when he fell into that bat cave, he could have never been called Batman. He could have been called something really off putting, like Superman.

Accountability is about relationships. It's the first honest intention for an addict re-entering society on a functional level. It is a process, like all of this. It takes time, and it's a lot of steps. But one honest truth is that once you are sober, it happens pretty naturally, and God helps you fairly quickly.

Chapter 5

LIFE IS...RELATIONSHIPS

THE GREATEST RELATIONSHIP you can have in this life is with your higher power. At least that's what I'm told. It may be that the greatest relationship I have is with my wife, through my higher power, if that makes sense.

Addicts suck at relationships. Yet they are the number one tool in our recovery. I know I was overly selfish and some people say it's a selfish program—recovery programs—but that's utter nonsense. It is a selfless program. Relationships have to be prioritized, as does our thought process in those relationships. First comes our sobriety, our higher power, ourselves, our spouses, our family, and the rest. Some argue the place of a higher power and sobriety, but that's the order I like to put it in. The whole reason we have that order is to ensure we can be functional for our spouses, family and friends. I'm told work should be on the bottom of that list, but it is a solid on the list nonetheless.

Before I met my wife, when I first sobered up, it seemed like all my relationships were scattered. Nobody really wanted to have a relationship with me, and I felt like a leper in medieval times. I had to work really hard to obtain and restore relationships, and I still don't have very many today. That's because my relationships today are more conscious. They're not based on flattery, lust, want, or greed. They are genuine; the number has gone down, but the quality has gone up.

To be properly engaged in a relationship, you must care for another as you would care for yourself. That's why you can't love others if you don't love yourself. If you don't respect yourself by abusing substances, you cannot respect others. You can't give what you don't have, and even though most relationships aren't 50/50 on a knowledge level, they are usually balanced out on a spiritual plain. For the most part, we're all just students and teachers. We typically have more to teach as we get older. Relationships are a constant evolution; sometimes they evolve into extinction, and that's okay because we usually only get a handful that are pertinent to our everyday well-being.

Teachers and students. Teachers are capable of being amazed by their students; in fact, they relish it. They relish seeing that dynamic at work. We cannot grow without each other, and God has given us each other, so we cannot survive without Him, without what He has given. Some argue He is the greatest teacher, so what do you think He's doing? He is reflecting upon Himself, in our journey, our decision, our choice. He's being amazed by us; He is relishing in our evolution and the ways in which we amaze Him. After all, we are made in His image; how do we make things better without starting with ourselves first?

So, for argument's sake, let me rephrase and say the greatest relationship you can have is with yourself. You have to be kind to yourself, love yourself, or all other relationships will fail. Love thyself first and you will learn to love all in your life equally. That is possibly the definition of perfect love. A love only God can attain, but is that not even more reason to strive for it? For balance? Harmony?

Balance within yourself cannot be achieved without harmony in all other relationships. So keep it simple. Start small. Start with your relationship with your addictions councilor, move onto the relationship with your sponsor, then your parents, your spouse, your children, and stop there. Limit your world; prioritize your life inwardly before expanding outwardly. Pick and choose. Decide. Commit to that which you can only sustain, that in which you can cope. Then you will begin to rebuild control within *your* life. But know you can never control anyone else's. You can guide your children, present the illusion of control so they feel safe, but you have to give them "control" of themselves as soon as they come of age.

Partnerships are an interesting topic. They only belong between you, God, and your spouse. Business partnerships are based on greed and ego, and can never be sustained. Partnerships are not about struggle. They are not about right or wrong. They are about compromise and good faith. They are an endeavor in which a bold few, it seems, can ever really commit. Divorce rates skyrocket due to relationships being based on unreal, selfish expectations. Anybody can say *I am*, but few people can say *we are*, and truly mean it. After three years, I find myself at that place with my wife. Why? Because I had faith she was the right thing for me. I compromised, I committed, I was honest, and I didn't cheat…even though I could have. We all can.

With media, it's hard. Everything is about me, myself, what I want, instantly. But where is that longing for something more. I know it exists because that's the exact emotion marketers sell you on. Even the majority of self-help books are rhetorical selfish, one-sided garbage; it's gotten that bad, and no one is getting to the point. The point is life is about each other. Not *your* feelings, or *your* thoughts, or *your* addiction. That's a part of it; those elements are a part of your life and your story. But the real legacy is what we leave behind—it is our children, our developed knowledge, our actions. That is the eternal; that is our God sense. The contribution. It is where we come from, and where we are going, universally. The point is knowing that purpose has found you today, and each and every day, for a beautiful reason.

That reason is love. Why? God is love. He is merciful and shows us reason and purpose, through good times and bad, so that we know love. So that we can teach love and let love reign, as He reigns. It is in our various relationships that we find love. We must love in order to experience the purpose of life. Sometimes love isn't enough, and all we have is life, but as long as we have life, we live to love again. It's cliché, but it's true. It's why Shakespeare wrote plays, why Patton marched through Europe. It's about obtaining love, protecting it, and always allowing it to reign victorious. It starts with ourselves, our God, and our spouse, and then it becomes so much more. It is our way of life. It is American, Canadian, British, Australian, Israeli. It's French and Italian and Spanish and Danish (that ones for my wife). It's western culture and Asian culture, but it isn't an extremist culture. It isn't based upon fear; it is the opposite of fear. It is reason. It is black and white, day and night, a line in the sand that very few can comprehend. It is an idea, a truth, a universal law, do unto others and never do wrong. You must know love to experience a healthy relationship. You must know love to understand your purpose. To know love is the purpose of relationships and the purpose of relationships is to pass love on.

Chapter 6

LIFE IS ... PURPOSE

WE ALL SEEK purpose, yet it all seems so misguided in our culture and media. The truth is media is designed to get you down on your knees and keep you there because it plays with your emotions of adequacy and entitlement.

Have you ever seen a gangster rapper without a sense of entitlement? A rock star? An actor? An athlete? Have you ever felt adequate compared to one of those people. Once you get paid, you're in the club, and once you're in the club, it becomes about keeping the other 99 percent, the 99 problems, down so you don't lose what you have. Can you imagine Taylor Swift giving all of her money to charity and starting over for the love of music? Playing county fairs and dive bars. No, you can't. But that's what she sells you on—love, false hope, being a good person. Stars all say it's for the love of acting, or the love of music, or the love of the game. But how many NHL superstars give up the game and go coach atom hockey where the real love of the game is. Very few. It's a business. Period. And it's a business of distorting kids' dreams, perceptions, and realities about what's really important in life. And it is destroying our future. It's not about values anymore. It's not the fact that they are athletes or rock stars or actors, it's the fact that they are held in such reverence that the majority of them do not hold themselves accountable to their status in life; they don't give back proportionately. It's about our kids thinking they are entitled to that reverence. It's about our children seeing and doing as our superstars, our "heroes," do rather than as God does. It's about claiming false idols.

For example, if you are in jail right now, locked down and under age, know that you being there hurts all of us collectively as a society. You have been recorded in society as another wrong. But think—what will you learn in your time behind bars? That wrong is right? How to be a better criminal? How to say, "Screw it, I'm getting drunk the day I get out of here"? Then you'll be listening to Jay-Z and slanging crack again, or whatever. You're thinking *Jay-Z made it, why can't I* as you destroy more lives in the process. Truth be told, Jay-Z, or whatever his name is, should be put in jail for influencing children to sell and do drugs. Millions of children. He should be handed consecutive life sentences. Instead, he's being embraced; he's buying basketball teams, and our society rewards him for perpetuating evil. Think about it. Is that what you want to be remembered for? The more a person is focused on evil, is addicted, is lost, the less likely he or she is to obtain your position in life. Fact: it's how you "get ahead." The more a person is concerned about his own survival, the less likely he is to be of value, after your position. Thus, distorting purpose. That's the game. That's the way of the streets. That's the way of business.

Are we all throw-aways? It seems so at times. We are all rolling down the pyramid of life so King Tut and his minions can sit at the top. But their way, the evil way, is not right. It is not correct; it is not a purpose-filled way. Our purpose must be a God-filled purpose. A merciful purpose. We must show mercy to receive it. We are the lowly so let us be low. Let us walk away and let their pyramid collapse from underneath them. I dare you, turn away from Satan and turn towards God. Some of the best people I know are former criminals, addicts, bikers, and veterans. It's who Jesus hung around with. Tax collectors, whores, the real people who lived life. If I am to learn anything, let me learn that I am not defined by my title. Our status does not define our purpose. All these circumstances you blame God for, that I blamed God for, are not of God; they are man-made. If society never gave you a chance, the least you can do is give yourself one. Where are all the good people? They're in church; they're in meetings; they are teaching and protecting our children. They're Sam Childers fighting in Africa for war-torn children. It's a movie, *Machine Gun Preacher*—watch it. The good people in this world are fighting for you. The problem is they are few and far between. They are not united, they are scattered in their own purpose. There is no great war to fight; there is no Hitler to kill. The heroes have disbanded, and with them, the society they created. Their children forgot; they didn't understand, and now we are left with idealists and sinners to guide our "purpose" driven lives. What a joke.

Purpose is essential to our being. It's about priorities, and you really have to ask yourself, what are yours? Mine is my family. My wife and daughter, in-laws and mother. That's what I can cope with. That's what I focus my time on. And that's all I need. I have dreams. Dreams of opening a rehab center for youth with a few friends of mine. But that's the extent of it. I dream of serving; I dream of helping. Not myself, but other people. God has a purpose for you, like any teacher does for a student. It takes a while to find your purpose, because true purpose is honest hope and honest desire…and it takes a while to get honest.

None of us ever asked for this. To be addicts, to be castaways. It was a hand dealt to us, but it was our choice to enter into the temptation, to play that hand. So, how are you going to amaze Him, what are you going to prove when your time comes. Are you going to say I chose evil so judge me justly? Did you say that to the judge? To your parents? My sponsor says heaven and hell are on earth—we create them; it's largely in our heads. Truth be told, it is. If we think positively, openly, and honestly, we do become good people. If we are negative, one-sided, and scared, we tend to create that hell, and it plays our minds and hearts. Fear affects our true purpose.

I have more fear today than I ever had when I was using. Why? I simply have more to lose. But I don't let it consume me. If you have ever watched *Star Wars* you will know it is a good parable for what I am talking about. Yoda says fear leads to anger, anger leads to hate, and hate leads to the dark side…. There couldn't be a truer statement. I was trapped in hate. I hated my mother; I hated my father; I hated God; I hated myself most of all. But when that broke, when I realized I needed help, when I asked for it, it all began to change. I could breathe again. I found courage instead of fear, love instead of anger, and hope in the place of hate. It takes *will* and backbone to stand up, not for your gang, but for yourself. To be a lone shepherd, in search of that everlasting flock, an everlasting legacy, it takes will.

People will always tell you what you are or are not in life. But it's up to you to listen. You decide; it's God's decision for you to decide; but know there is a correct decision. If you're losing, and only you know if you are, then what more do you have to lose? There is a way out of this competition our media has put in your head. It's called surrender. Surrender to your purpose. What has God put in your heart to achieve? Trust it. Earn it. Believe in your dreams. What do you want to accomplish? What is in your heart? Do you want to be a father? A husband? A wife? A mother? Do you want to see the world?

What will bring you heart glory? What do you dare to dream? Accomplish it, but be accountable for it. Be a rock star, but be accountable. If this book sells, half of my end is going to charity. That is a fact. That is my accountability to the gifts God has given me. It's 50/50, like anything else in life. Life is limitless, but it is not singular. Your purpose cannot be singular. It has to have multiple interactions, definitions, and outcomes. Everything you do affects someone else. Your purpose may be predetermined by God, but it is achieved by you. Your work, your blood, your sweat. And it's yours to give away, but you can't give away what you don't have. So let the entitled be jealous and let the adequate know their worth. We are all adequate, the entire 99 percent of us. The trick was to educate myself in the ways of the world before I made anymore poor decisions.

> Jesus said, "I am the Bread of Life. The person who aligns with me hungers no more and thirsts no more, ever. I have told you this explicitly because even though you have seen me in action, you don't really believe me. Every person the Father gives me eventually comes running to me. And once that person is with me, I hold on and don't let go. I came down from heaven not to follow my own whim but to accomplish the will of the One who sent me.
>
> —JOHN 6:37 THE MESSAGE

So find your purpose, don't stop until you do. Hunt it down and become who you were meant to be, not just another name scratched in the paint of a holding cell. Believe. Believe in your dreams, if nothing else, because every purpose is meaningful to life and every life is purposeful.

Chapter 7

LIFE IS ... AMBITION

When you grow up you tend to get told that the world is the way it is and your life is just to live your life inside the world. Try not to bash into the walls too much. Try to have a nice family life, have fun, save a little money. That's a very limited life. Life can be much broader once you discover one simple fact: Everything around you that you call life was made up by people that were no smarter than you. And you can change it, you can influence it... Once you learn that, you'll never be the same again.
—STEVE JOBS

AMBITION HAS DESTROYED more people than any drug or drink. It's trampled, bullied, and cheated, even killed those who put it above others and their own well-being. That's because it was misguided. Ambition is defined as a strong desire to do or achieve something, typically requiring determination and hard work.

Hard work and determination are typically foreign subjects to us. What the definition doesn't say is that ambition requires discipline to be successful.

We all have ambitions; I know I do. For a time I wanted to make music for a living. I practiced and wrote songs, sang, and played guitar; it's what I wanted. But people often told me my songwriting was better than my singing and that I should write again; it's been so long. Truthfully, I wrote a little bit in high school—always poetry and songs. But my ambition for music was blinded; it was unrealistic. I didn't have the raw talent in music that I did for literature. For years I would bang away on my Gibson thinking *I'm doing it, I'm getting better*, all the while my wife, mother, and friends were shaking their heads.

I knew what I wanted, and I tied it into my addiction. I said, "I can't play music if I am not high." In fact, it all began because I got high. I was nineteen, sitting outside my home and heard a Blue Rodeo concert in the distance. The cheering, the drums, I thought *Wouldn't it be nice if people would cheer for me, if people loved me*. So I went and bought a guitar. Then I got good at writing songs and received validation. I turned that validation into contempt for others and myself, and I used that validation as another excuse for my addiction. Then one day my audience went from bar flies to patients in a mental hospital, and I wasn't so cool anymore. So I guess, now, my ambition has changed a little.

Without ambition, people wouldn't accomplish great things like Steve Jobs did, but the point I am trying to make with my music story is that you don't have to be great. You can be average. You can have a niche, a hobby, and excel at that. That's all it is to me today, an artistic release. God gives us all certain gifts. You really have to let your ambition find you, and ground you upon your strengths, your successes. And it starts with sobriety. Developing a God sense. Surrendering control. Asking for help. Being honest. Becoming accountable. Developing relationships. Finding a purpose. These are all first steps in undertaking your ambition. There must be a method to your madness, as there is to mine. If I am ambitious towards anything, it should first be towards making myself a better person. Because without an inward ambition, the external ambition falls short.

A moral ambition is key. It is existential to do the right thing, and it's about doing the right thing all the time. That's where we begin. That's where I began. I look at my priorities—sobriety, God, myself, my partner, my child, my family, my work. How do I conduct myself in my daily affairs? I must balance these personal priorities before I can undertake my life's ambition because, believe it or not, these personal priorities are my life's ambition. They're 90 percent of it. The rest, the achievement, it's just fluff. This 10 percent simply makes me look appealing to others.

A moral compass is at the heart of all ambition and life's undertaking. The people who stay true to the compass truly succeed in life. Success is measured on various levels by different people. One obvious eyesore is the desire for wealth, but what if you look past monetary gain, forget the one percent. What's left? A decent job that you enjoy? Family? It's really about how we spend our time. That defines how we are remembered. Not by the masses, but the ones we love. If you are a teacher, like my wife plans to be, realistically you get two and a half months off a year, you're home every night, and your salary (here in Canada) maxes out at around $80,000 to $90,000 a year. What more could you ask for? What more do you need? You really have to ask yourself where your ambitions lie.

Ambition is a picture of where you want to be. My picture is a single family home in a good neighborhood, two newer cars, a dog, a cat, and maybe two more kids. It's basically the Simpsons, but it's a lot different from what it used to be. I thought I would be famous, or at least write songs for famous people, live in New York, be a playboy in a nicely sized Manhattan loft, drinking martinis all day. I was delusional. Yet it caused me to write great songs that I had no idea how to market. So I am not saying that ambition can't be productive, I am just saying my misguided ambition was destructive to me.

Ambition changes, it's natural; it grows and develops with your character, personality, and influences. So when Steve Jobs says what he does about life found in the quote at the top of the chapter, know that it all starts with a nice family life, having a little fun, and saving a little money. You don't bang the walls before you own the walls your about to bang. You don't have the support to change life and influence it without a family, and you sure don't have a little fun while building the most dominate corporate empire the world has ever seen. Life is about choices. Know you can choose not to play *their* game. You don't have to be a slave, serving money or substances as your god. You can choose to be happy.

Chapter 8

LIFE IS . . . FORGIVENESS

THE HARDEST THING I have had to learn, hands down, is how to forgive myself. Forgiveness is deep, like an ocean. We really have to descend to the reef to understand all the waves we encounter upon the surface.

The first time I went surfing in Hawaii, I got up. The entire session, I got up. My instructor would tell me when to paddle and when to stand, but the balance was all me. It was natural, like forgiveness, it just takes a bit of instruction.

My Big Book was my best friend during my early sobriety. I would just open it up and read. Now I do that to my Bible, or other spiritual works. My spirituality has grown deeper, and with it, my forgiveness. My Bible is not my religious connection; it is my spiritual connection. My religion simply helps me understand it.

It was easy to forgive others in comparison to myself. I had inner resentments that crippled my emotions. I was a cadet and planned to join the military when the war started. I was scouted for intelligence work but never joined due to my addiction. I carried that guilt for a long time. My friends had joined; I saw the fighting on the news, and I could have made a difference, but I never did. By the time I had the courage to join, my medical record prevented me from doing so.

It's funny the way things work out. If you had asked me at fourteen if I'd ever tried drugs, I would have said, "Yeah, I tried drugs, but I am never doing them again because I want to succeed in life." But what is success other than actualized aspirations. Forgiving myself for not being man enough to chase what I wanted when it was right in front of me, that was the hard part. Facing ourselves, our paths, our choices and destinies, and coming to terms with our reality, that's where forgiveness begins.

It is okay that I am here today, in my circumstance, because this is where I am meant to be. My shortcomings are not the definition of my character. My character is the definition of my ability to overcome those shortcomings.

Jesus forgave. He forgave those who put Him to death. God, through Jesus, forgave us, our original sin, and our imperfection. The student and the teacher. We are not our parents; we are not that which came before us, nor that which is ahead. We are here, now, in actuality. To forgive is to realize the past is out of our control. If we were wronged by our parents, know that the action is out of their control, that time has passed. Forgiveness is natural because forgiveness is about peace, and peace is a natural state for people. If you can forgive others, you can forgive yourself. You forgive others with time, distance, and reflection. You forgive others by knowing their imperfection and comparing it to yours because we are likewise imperfect and must therefore forgive. The only perfect things in this life are given by God; the act of forgiveness is perfection in his eyes.

Once you have forgiven repeatedly, it becomes easier and easier until you come to the place where you no longer feel spite towards those who say or do offensive things towards you. My wife and I are kind of that way with each other. We can push buttons, and then, boom! But it hasn't happened in a really long time. Forgiveness leads to tolerance. Probably because forgiveness is such an emotional undertaking, we tend to defer to tolerance, especially if it is someone we love. It all comes back to inner harmony and balance. When things are out of whack, we are out of whack. It affects everything, everyone. When my wife has had a bad day, and I speak with her, for some odd reason, I begin to have a bad day too. The best policy regarding forgiveness is thoughtful honesty. Consideration, empathy, or sympathy for what the other is going through. When it comes to self-forgiveness and ourselves, we must most importantly share what we are going through with another person to make that necessary, healing, back-and-forth dialogue possible. Like I said before, trained, educated, successful people are who I tend to bounce things off of. It's important to have that support network relevant and up-to-date on your current situations to be successful. It is essential in order to be able to work out forgiveness in your mind and heart.

Forgiveness is action. It is taking myself out for a Starbucks, treating myself to my favorite movie or book. It is about me accepting an apology and showing an act of good faith. Taking that extra step to ensure a good relationship between others and myself. Without a relationship, there is no point to forgive. It's better to forget, especially if that other person was unhealthy for your life.

The only relationships I regret not being mended were those of my extended family. I am still struggling with that. Neither side has reached out because neither side has forgiven. They judged, and I judged them for judging. Heavy shame. It's the hardest when it is family; it's the hardest to forget those good memories. Maybe one day, but not today. Maybe one Christmas we will all be united, but not this one. Time has a way of healing all wounds, all hearts. Sometimes people just need a little more time than others. Sometimes it's simply meant to be memories. Only Christ can change hearts; only Christ can teach us the value of each other, and that's really what forgiveness is all about. There is no point to forgive if you do not forget.

Looking to the Bible, where Jesus forgave Peter and gave him his flock, allows me to see the totality of the entire act of forgiveness. Peter stayed close and denied Jesus three times where the other apostles scattered. And this is a total rip off of my pastor, but he was close enough to be a part of the passion, to be there with Jesus, while far enough away to survive. He stepped out of the boat and walked on water with Jesus. He had the faith, even though he "failed" when tested at times. Sometimes failing really isn't failing because it is part of a higher purpose God has planned for us. And as an addict, that is something I really had to believe in. It's about God forgiving us. And that's a forgiveness I really didn't think I had, or at least didn't feel, until I held my daughter for the first time in my arms. Perhaps I had some form of God's forgiveness, but I never had his merciful grace until that day. I really felt it then.

I felt like my past was behind me.

Chapter 9

LIFE IS . . . EACH OTHER

IF YOU WATCH many war movies, you soon realize it's about the guy next to you. It is how we survive. Our human sociology is based upon interdependence.

Chances are someone has let you down. It's why you let yourself down. It's why you chose substances or money over accountability. We all are accountable to each other. It is all about each other. Relationships, desires, purpose. It's all intertwined. My wife and daughter are essential to my survival, as I am to theirs. We are all meant to be co-dependent, interdependent anyone who tells you otherwise is wrong. When you find another person worth living for, you have truly found God's design working within your life.

When I was a kid, a teenager, my greatest hole was a non-existent father. I never knew my dad. I knew things about him. That he was ex-military, a biker, a musician. But not much more. I was told things, and I had a picture of him at one point in my life. I saw his military eagle tattoo on his arm; I saw his black vest and his long, black, curly hair, and I knew that was my dad. I could never find him. He was elusive, or dead. It left me with a lot of questions and with one big excuse for not facing life. I burned that picture and damned him to hell. But I always wished I hadn't. I long to see his face because that was all I had, an image. I don't know if I have brothers or sisters, grandparents. It's all a blur to me. It's still a hole; he's one person I will never have, but that hole taught me the most about my value and importance in regards to watching over my family.

Life is each other because life is the love we have for each other. I still love my dad. I love the thought of him. I am still overly kind to any biker, veteran, or military personnel. I am shown that fatherly love through them because they see how I look at them. You know that part about standing up for what you believe in, well, you can't find a better example than within your parents. Especially if they tried the best they could.

My sponsor was military, my other close friend in the program is an old biker and between the two of them, they always give me sound, fatherly advice. They're both coming from two different worlds, but oddly enough, their principles are the same. I don't judge their paths; I accept them.

God will always stand up for you. I think of Him as my father. I am learning from Him as a father, and becoming a better father because of Him. And I'm relishing the thought of amazing Him as His son. Pleasing Him. Helping myself. What will I choose next. Life's a choose-your-own-adventure book, but my higher power seems to be turning the pages.

I remember my mom and I having movie nights when I was young. I love my mom! We would pick a neutral drama, sometimes love, sometimes war. We would make a big bowl of popcorn and just sit next to each other on the couch, enjoying the story and each other's company. And what good is a story if you don't have someone to share it with? My wife and I do the same now, in bed or in our loungers. I like to think I would have never known that intimacy if it wasn't for my mom. When I was a kid, I loved cuddling with my mom. If our mothers teach us how to love, our fathers teach us how to stand. All this time I thought my father was teaching me to stand alone, but now I realize his absence was teaching me to stand with God.

"Rest in me, my child. Give your mind a break from planning and trying to anticipate what will happen. Pray continually, asking My Spirit to take charge....Remember you are on a journey with me...who sustains you moment by moment."[1]

Without each other, from a sociological standpoint, we would not exist. Nothing we know today would be here. The good or the bad. Which are you focused on? Blaming the world for your decisions. The external influencing the internal? We have each other, so we can learn from each other. Jesus had twelve apostles and a family. He just didn't bust in saying He was the Son of God, He had a circle, within a circle, within a circle. Chances are He followed Jewish customs of that day. He was just as much human as He was God, and He obeyed his birth parents. He had a trade, and He never really started trouble until He was prepared to make His point, until the timing was right. To understand the "myth," according to non-believers, you have to understand the point in history it occurred.

Jesus made His life about "each other" because that's what He was taught as a child. It was God's will to make Him Mary and Joseph's child because they were humble and loved God. Jesus was taught a humble existence for each other and by each other. And that is what He

---

1 Sarah Young, *Jesus Calling* (Nashville: Thomas Nelson, 2012), 169.

reciprocated. Joseph, Mary, and the Jewish community taught Him how to live a Godly life, and He taught us.

I think it was Glenn Beck, whom I saw in an interesting clip, talking about the man at the pool at Bethesda, where Jesus healed him. He questioned what that man did once he was healed. He answered that the man quit begging, married, and raised a family, as was commonplace in those times. He got on with his life. And that is what I, as an addict, had to do when my time came. I got up, got on with it, and made it about the gal next to me. I married and started a family. Got a sense of community and made it about "each other." That beggar probably became a Christian once Christ was crucified. For the life of me I can't remember his name (I'm still learning my Bible), but I'm guessing he probably did a lot of great things in his community without ever once worrying if his name would be remembered.

Chapter 10

LIFE IS . . . FAMILY

I KNOW I JUST talked about each other and my family, and have throughout the book, but I can't emphasize this point enough. It's important, critical. Your inner group sustains your inner worth. Family isn't a gang. It isn't your homies. It is your blood. Your woman. Your man. Your kids. Period.

Not all families are all they're cracked up to be. All families are dysfunctional to some extent. But my main goal in life is to build and sustain a functional family. It goes back to our legacy. What we pass on. That bond between our wife or husband, kids, and God. Our primary purpose should be the well-being of each other, our unit. Focus on that family, and then expand. Sacrifice, build, and worship God for your family. If you are not hitched, let God help choose your mate. Be honest; trust your gut because most people desire to be with someone.

I met my wife online. I simply changed my profile from a guy who wanted to get laid to a guy who wanted a family. We were a 90 percent match according to that website, and I would have to agree with their accuracy still to this day. See, women are usually honest. Most women want a strong man, but a lot of strong men have trouble being loyal. It's because they are actually not strong men; they simply appear to be strong to compensate for their fear of commitment and life. The strongest men are usually the quiet ones who don't shoot off their mouth. Those are the guys you have to watch out for in a fight. Those are the guys who, in my family, are welcome to come date my daughter...when she's of an appropriate age.

Family is special, and you have to protect it above all else, even if that means you have to protect it from itself. For me it's a constant juggle between my in-laws and my mother, and my wife and myself. It seems no one sees eye to eye. My father in-law is telling me to get a real job; my mom is telling me to go to school; everybody wants to tell me what I am and am not, what I can and cannot do, simply because they all care. In their own ways, they all care about my wife and me, and of course our daughter. That is often what family is, misguided love. Even in the midst of hate, the one commonality is we all love each other, and that is the kind of unit God intended. An unbreakable bond of emotion. Passion. Family will always love family.

Addicts are never perfect at family life. It's why we go to meetings, meet sponsors, and make friends. The old timers, they usually know a thing or two about enjoying that time at home. They can relax and let things come as they may, but they're not afraid to crack the whip. And that's the kind of dad I strive to be. Gentle yet firm. You cannot be passive and you cannot be controlling; it works for a time, but when I started to rebel, the only thing that saved me was the fact that I knew right from wrong. It is the only reason I am here today. To be treated fairly is the best thing we could ask for, and that is really the only thing we should accept from our family members.

The family I knew as a kid was really a community. It had points of focus. My grandparents, my great aunts and uncles, and their families. Even my great, great uncles and aunts were part of the norm. It seems like everybody in my family lives until one-hundred. There were multiple farms that my extended family owned and places, businesses, in town and in the city. At one point in time, half of my town's main street was owned by a family member. My family has politicians, millionaires, and very influential people within it . . . and I was expected to live up to the hype.

I was an honor student and a cadet with honors; I coached sports teams; I played sports; I was a lifeguard; I counselled at a summer camp; basically, I looked really good on paper and to my family, but I was a wreck inside. I longed for that dad, so I started to rebel. In little ways. I would skip Sunday dinner and get stoned, or miss Saturday morning breakfast at my grandparents because I was hung over. My family really held me together through most of high school until my Baba passed. And like I said earlier, then it all fell apart. But truth be told, I was already falling apart. Submitting to the pressure. When I went to college at seventeen a couple of hours away from home, I lost all accountability.

Looking back, I learned that I crack under pressure. But it's not a bad thing. I've learned everybody cracks; we are only designed to take on so much. But I cracked because I was spoon fed a reality that did not exist. Not mindfully, but my family sheltered me from the realities of this world because they cared, and I believe that is the most dangerous thing a family can do to a teenager. Especially church/homeschool/small town families. It is dangerous to not know that "dark" side of life. It should be taught in our schools, churches, and homes. "This is where you end up, if…" How would society thrive without that loser, that competition? Imagine.

That being said, I am still a firm believer in reality. Disillusionment and entitlement have killed more kids than handguns and grenades.

Chapter 11

LIFE IS ... REST

SLEEP IS SOMETHING I could do all day long. Life is about hard honest work, but it is also about hard honest sleep, down time, relaxation.

Rest is what gives us the ability to face our day-to-day lives. I typically run all summer and sleep all winter, like a bear. Down time is the greatest time we can give to ourselves, especially in recovery. I don't know how many movies I went through in early recovery, but I have a bookcase of DVDs to prove that I did. Movies like *August Rush*, *Kingdom of Heaven* (directors cut), *Machine Gun Preacher*. I'd watch them over and over again, rebuilding who I was. Nurturing that longing in my heart. In *Kingdom of Heaven*, my favorite line is " What man is man if he does not make the world better." It was something I began to live by; there was a truth in it that, one I understood. I found these creeds, these lessons, in rest, and I carried them into my daily life. In *August Rush*, I saw a love story and a child, so pure and innocent, I knew one day I wanted it for myself. In *Machine Gun Preacher*, I saw the true story of a man who turned his life around and gave it to the Lord, and I wanted that. *Rocky Balboa* touched on my sense of morality and manhood, and I longed for that—that trust he found within himself. Even God rested after six days of work.

Today, my down time is often spent in TV shows or playing guitar. As an addict, I do what I have to do to unwind soberly. I go for breakfast with my sponsor; I play an ever fabulous game of tent with my daughter. I watch *Friends* with my wife... over and over again. When I'm not working my steps, I am still working my steps because I am always improving my conscious contact with God as I understand Him—step eleven. I understand him through my family and peers.

We can do all we can do and then we can be. I can be with my family, myself; my friends and not be overcome by anxiety or worry. Resting is about separation of work and play. If we are not working, ideally we should be in rest, or at least enjoying our undertaking of the day. Stress is what perpetuated my addiction, self-induced stress. That is the majority of it when you think about it. For me, it was about putting myself in a position in life that I could handle, somewhere I could cope. I still get anxiety to this day, but I say in my head, I pray *I give up Jesus, I give up; help me. I give up.* And He does. It's my mantra—surrender—and He gives me rest from myself.

Like a hangover, when you sober up, I highly recommend sleep. Ten, twelve hours a night. It restores your brain; it lifts the fog, and it feels great. When I get off work early at six or seven, I'm in bed by eight. I sleep until four-thirty and get on with my following day. I make up wherever I can for those five-hour nights I so often get. It's why I always burnout by fall. When first snow hits, I sleep for days, a week, straight until noon.

For me, my rest is spent with family. It's how I choose to re-charge. My daughter, being nearly two, can be a handful, but she's way too cute to ever be angry with. My downtime today is church on Sundays and meetings on

Wednesday nights. Rest is about having fun, together, as much as it is alone. There's two different kinds of rest: active rest and passive rest. It's like when Rocky Balboa picks out Punchy from the pound; he's just lying there in the corner and Rocky says, "That's a smart dog; he's conserving energy." That's what I have to do sometimes, be a dog. Play with the family or lay in the corner. I have to do whatever I must do so I can go out and heard our sheep the next day, and do it properly. Rocky really does remind me of Jesus, waiting for the opportune moment to make His move. To win the battle. Conserving energy and waiting until life quits hitting; to get the left hook in on it. To make your mark. That is how winning is done. With consistent rest and opportune moments. And then a little more rest. They always say you're only as good as your last round, and you're only as good as the guy in your corner. Well, the guy in my corner makes it a pretty comfortable corner.

Chapter 12

LIFE IS . . . PASSING IT ON

WE PASS LIFE, the details about life, from parent to child. Friend to friend. We share our experience in hope that it may one day help others. The beauty lies not in passing it on, but in watching it be received.

Change is hard. Where you are now is not where you will be in five or ten years. A number of different things can impact you between now and then. If you can breathe, you can love; if you can love, you can fight, and if you can fight, you can believe in something and allow it to become bigger than yourself. If you can love and fight for yourself, you can believe in God and allow His purpose for you to become greater than your own.

People will always tell you this or that, but you are your own greatest enemy by trying to decipher the truth without the discernment of God.

I just ask Him for help.

For me, this book is what I pass on to my daughter; when she is old enough and mature enough, I will tell her my story. I will say, "I did this, and this is what I learnt from it." I will show her exactly where my knowledge comes from. I will pass on to her how I obtained my knowledge of how to become a better person. My wife is on this journey with me: she is the one reading and editing this book as I go along. Other than the occasional swearing (which may now be edited), she's on board; she thinks I'm doing the right thing.

So, I challenge you, put your story down, even for your-self. Tell it in the rooms; give your testimony at church. See if you attract a worthy life with your honesty. Youth groups, support groups, church groups. Find your wife or husband; if you've found her or him, rediscover them again. Discover your life and possibilities. Dare to dream larger. Be impactful. Take this book, put it away, and read it again when times get tough. Use my story to understand that no matter how bad it gets, God will always be there. He was for me. Even when I didn't know it.

Passing it on is about Grace in your life. I received God's grace even when I didn't know He was there. I never killed anybody; I was never convicted of anything more than a misdemeanor, I had guns in my face, but none of them went off. I was at a point where I hated God, but He still had my back because I am alive today. If you are reading this, you are alive today, and He has your back. I remember the psych wards, the jail cells, the cold nights on the streets. Every day. It's there, and it doesn't go away. But every day, I wake up and see my daughter, my wife, and my Bible, and I am reminded that I survived my own self-destruction. God has a purpose for me, and I intend to discover it because I have seen hell; I have lived it. I cre-ated it. And today I know the truth. That hell does not have to be my reality, not when there is a heaven here on earth. It's in the words of the Gospel. They're instructions. They are here because they are intended for you to build your life around. They, along with the Big Book are God's blue-prints for your own personal design, and they are good for you. Trained, educated, successful people are who I build my life around today; and I myself am surviving, slowly growing up, but I would have never, ever known today, if I hadn't been humbled *multiple* times and *learned* from those lessons.

"He who is slow to anger is better than the mighty, And he who rules his spirit, than he who captures a city" (Proverbs 16:32).

"I call heaven and earth to witness against you today, that I have set before you life and death, the blessing and the curse. So choose life in order that you may live, you and your descendants" (Deuteronomy 30:19).

Amen. And Godspeed on your journey.

ABOUT THE AUTHOR

Coming from a small town, country upbringing, Suede Frunchak was raised in a place where his ancestors worked the land for well over a century. An honor student in grade school Suede found his downfall into addiction shortly after graduating high school. Addicted for nearly a decade, he began a true and honest recovery at twenty-five-years-old. Married shortly after, Suede is now a husband, a father of a two-year-old, and nearly thirty, looking back. With a strong passion and desire to help others, to redeem his lost years, his family, and his friends, he began work on *Life Is...* shortly after his twenty-ninth birthday. In seeking Christ, he has sought himself a better person and through *Life Is...* strives to pass on the message of recovery to the youth of our nations. Born a fourth generation Canadian, he has intended the book for not only the youth of North America, but for whomever will listen. Seeing drugs as an epidemic, an industry, and a culture, Suede is attempting, with his testimony, to make fighting this epidemic his life's work. With the help of God, he prays for a youth recovery ministry to develop and center on this work. He hopes that the Spirits work through *Life Is...* may be his cornerstone in which to build this ministry and begin a recovery in those who are most precious to God, our children, and our future. He intends to pass on the same mercy and care he received from the people who saved his life. To pass on that same defining grace he received from the kind Lord, who took pity on his soul.

CONTACT THE AUTHOR

You may contact the author via email at:

Life.is.author@gmail.com